"This large book takes a look at how Jesus might have lived in the first century. It shows primary grade as well as preschool children that Jesus was a child just as they are, but that he grew up in a different world. Foods, clothing, homes were not like those of today. Play, prayer, and feast days were different, too.

"All of the crafts are suited for school or home use."

Edward O'Meara
Catholic Sentinel

"This book shows children in preschool and primary grades that Jesus was a child much like them. It gives them the sense of the differences between the world that Jesus grew up in and the world today. Specific descriptions of food, homes, clothing, work, play, prayer, and feasts introduce children to Jesus' world. The book contains a historical background for the teacher; questions and discussion starters that connect the biblical and modern world; crafts, games, and songs that suggest experiences that Jesus might have had."

Book World

"Designed to satisfy the curiosity of young children regarding the early life of Jesus, this handbook of stories, crafts, and activities for preschool and primary grades can help parents and religion teachers make Jesus come alive for their children. It does this with historical explanations of first-century Jewish customs and discussion questions that relate the biblical world to our own."

Extension Magazine

"*When Jesus Was Young* will delight teachers of children in kindergarten through fifth grade with stories, crafts, and activities to help them understand that 'Jesus was a child who grew and learned and worked and played, much as they do.' As a supplement to a text, or as the basis for a special teaching unit on the child Jesus, this book fills the need for an early childhood teaching tool."

Pat Durbin
Catholic Times

"This is the most complete book of its kind I have ever seen. The descriptions and activities should arouse the senses and capture the imagination of students. It is an excellent resource for readying students for their study of Scripture. MacClennan has developed activities that neophyte as well as more experienced catechists can use effectively in the classroom.

"One of the highlights of the book is the generous use of the 'Making Connections' portion of the teacher's pages. It's one thing to enter into a bit of the everyday world of Jesus and quite another to assist the students in connecting that remote time and culture to the student's present experience. This effective tool can aid students to accept Jesus as a real person and to connect the real person of Jesus to their life experiences now. Bravo, MacClennan."

William T. Krumm, M.A.
Director of Religious Education
Cincinnati

"*When Jesus Was Young: Stories, Crafts and Activities for Children* is an excellent text. The activities will go a long way toward developing positive attitudes in our children toward Jews and Judaism."

Eugene Fisher
NCCB Secretariat on
Ecumenical and Interreligious Affairs

WHEN JESUS WAS YOUNG

Stories, Crafts, and Activities for Children

Carole MacClennan

XXIII
TWENTY-THIRD PUBLICATIONS
Mystic, Connecticut

Illustrations by William Baker

Second printing 1993

Twenty-Third Publications
P.O. Box 180
185 Willow Street
Mystic, CT 06355
(203) 536-2611
800-321-0411

ISBN 0-89622-485-6
Library of Congress Catalog Card No. 91-65005

To
My mother and father
who showed me God's steadfast love

CONTENTS

Note to Parents and Teachers

The full-page illustrations on pages 7, 17, 25, 33, 41, 49, 57, and 65 may be used for coloring. If you wish to have your children use them in this way, permission is granted to duplicate these pages.

WHEN JESUS WAS YOUNG

WHEN JESUS WAS YOUNG
Introduction

No one knows, of course, exactly what Jesus did when he was a child. Archaeologists and historians have made it possible, however, for us to have an understanding of what life was probably like for a young Jewish boy living in first-century Galilee.

I am convinced it's necessary to pass on this information to children for a number of reasons. Once, at the beginning of Lent, a five year old said to me, "Gee, seems like Jesus was just 'borned' and already he's dying!" That observation illustrates how a child's mind processes words very literally. A child who thinks the Babe in the manger suddenly becomes the Man at Easter has a difficult time understanding that Jesus was truly one of us. We can help students become Christians who know Jesus personally by first helping them to understand that Jesus was a child who grew and learned and worked and played, much as they do. Knowing that Jesus was like them will help children believe they can be like him.

Specific historical detail can answer questions such as, "What did Jesus eat? What did his house look like? What did he wear?" With this kind of information the child can perceive of Jesus as a real person. Familiarity with historical detail promotes "Bible readiness," since it gives the child an understanding of words and situations that are used in Hebrew and Christian scripture.

Many writers since Vatican II have pointed out that in order to understand Jesus and his teachings, it is imperative to understand his life as a Jew. This book invites students to take a first step toward that understanding. And by presenting information about Jesus' Jewish upbringing, this book will in some small way encourage teachers to become instruments of healing so needed in Jewish-Christian relations.

When Jesus Was Young is designed to be used easily by busy people. Each chapter contains historical background and a brief chart that sums up facts at a glance, a read-to-me page that presents historical detail on a child's level, ideas for discussion, and activities developed to give students experiences similar to the ones Jesus might have had.

Teachers can choose to do all or some of the suggested activities. The activities from one chapter can be used with activities from another. For example, many activities in the "Food" chapter will fit into the "Work" chapter; "Musical Instruments" ("Play" chapter) can be used for the "Praise Parade" ("Feast of Weeks" chapter); wood shavings made in "Carpenter Shop" ("Work" chapter) can be put into "Leather Purse" ("Clothes" chapter). Please note that none of the activities for "Shabbat," "Sukkot," or "Shavuat" are meant to duplicate Jewish ritual. They simply adapt elements from these festivals to give a hint of experiences Jesus might have had.

This book can be used in many ways: as a supplement to a lesson in an existing religious education curriculum; as the basis for a unit on the child Jesus; to direct an on-going activity, such as a once-a-week or once-a-month lesson on the child Jesus; as background material for a vacation Bible school; or as a resource for children's liturgies.

May your students enjoy learning about the child Jesus and may they never want to stop learning about him!

FOOD
Teacher's Page—Historical Background

When Jesus lived in Galilee, food was simple but plentiful. Farmers produced wheat and barley, olives, grapes, figs, dates, apricots, pomegranates, melon, lettuce, beans, cucumbers, onions, and a variety of herbs. Many families kept a goat and chickens, insuring a supply of milk, cheese, butter, yogurt, eggs, and meat. Honey was available year-round. Fish and fowl were common, but beef and lamb were eaten only on special occasions.

A major part of a woman's day was spent preparing food. Every morning the wife baked bread, first grinding wheat or barley with a mortar and pestle or hand mill, then mixing it with water, salt, and a piece of fermented dough saved from the day before. She would knead the dough, let it rise, and shape it into flat, round loaves which she would bake in the communal clay oven. Barley, cheaper and heartier than wheat, was the grain most used by the poor.

The wife also milked the goat and made butter, cheese, and yogurt. Butter was made by putting milk in a goatskin bag, suspending the bag from a tripod made of three poles pushed into the ground, and punching the bag until the milk turned to butter.

Since storage methods were poor, the wife made a trip to the local marketplace each day.

Foods were usually boiled or stewed in a large pot and could be seasoned with salt, onion, garlic, mint, dill, corriander, rue, or mustard.

Breakfast was usually a small meal. It might have been a few nuts and raisins or a lit-

GALILEE

tle bread, some olives or cheese, or dried grain. This meal might be eaten on the run or carried to work and eaten mid-morning or mid-day. Supper was a more substantial meal consisting of bread, olives, vegetables, and watered wine. It could have included stew, eggs, cheese, butter, fruits, and nuts. Supper was eaten at the end of a long work day. The family members would wash their hands, pray, and gather around common bowls into which they would dip the fingers of their right hands to partake of the food. Sauces were scooped up with chunks of bread, which was always broken into pieces, never sliced.

Supper was the one time of day when the family members could come together, relax, and share each other's company, thus nourishing not only their bodies but also the strong Jewish family unit. During this time the father would retell stories about their Hebrew ancestors and teach his sons the rules and observances necessary to become a faithful Jew. A benediction ended the meal.

Eating Customs

No forks, knives, or spoons
Individuals dipped right hand into pots
Food eaten from common pots
Bread broken, not sliced

Common Foods

wheat or barley bread	porridge	grapes
olives	eggs	milk
cheese	yogurt	beans
cucumbers	figs	dates
apricots	pomegranates	melon
walnuts	almonds	pistachios
fish	wild fowl	honey
vinegar	wine	onion
herbs		

FOODS JESUS LIKED

What do you think it would be like to eat your meals without a fork, knife, or spoon? You might think that sounds messy, but when Jesus was growing up, people didn't eat with forks, knives, or spoons! So Jesus used a chunk of bread the way you might use a fork or spoon to "capture" his food.

Mary took hard barley grain and crushed it into soft flour. She used the flour to make bread for Jesus. She milked the goat and made butter, cheese, and yogurt from the milk.

Some foods Jesus ate are the same as foods you might eat, like grapes, lettuce, or eggs. Some foods Jesus ate might be foods you've never tasted, like goat's milk, barley bread, or pomegranates. For dessert, Jesus might have had raisins, figs, dates, walnuts, or almonds. Or maybe he dipped his bread into sweet, sticky honey!

Jesus' family ate supper together after working all day. They were happy to relax and share food, prayer, stories, and fun.

Teacher's Page
Making Connections

What activities could stimulate students' senses of smell and taste?

Imagine the child Jesus tasting, smelling, touching the foods he ate. Think of the warm fresh goat's milk, the smell of barley bread baking in the oven, the sticky honey on a crusty piece of bread, a tangy bite of cool cheese, the chewy sweetness of dried dates, the dripping juiciness of ripe melon.

Jesus saw farmers scatter seed and wait for plants to appear. This could have taught him about trust. He watched Mary mix the old and new dough together and set it to rise. This might have taught him about patience. At supper he listened as Joseph retold the stories of their ancestors. From this he might have learned faithfulness.

How can food be used to strengthen the family unit?

Discussion / Activity Starters

Jesus and his family ate with their fingers from a big bowl. What foods do you eat with your fingers?

With whom did Jesus share his meals? With whom do you share food? When? Where?

How do you think Jesus helped Mary prepare food? How can you help with meal time at home?

Do you think Jesus thanked Mary for making good food for him? How can you thank the people who make food for you?

Jesus' family thanked God for their food. Can you make up a prayer to say at meal time?

Activities

Crushing Barley

Materials: Two flat stones 4" or 5" across. Barley (found in grocery or health food store).

Procedure: Take turns. Place a few grains of barley between stones. Pound or crush into flour.

Child should: Feel finished product. Compare to original.

Child learned: Flour is crushed grain. Flour is used to bake bread. Mary might have used barley flour to bake bread for her family.

Making Connections: Where do you get bread? What kind? Does your family use flour to bake things? What?

Proofing Yeast

Materials: Small bowl, 2 dish towels, mixing spoon, 1/4 cup warm water, 1 T dry yeast, several drops of honey, piece of bread showing air holes made by yeast.

Procedure: Sprinkle yeast on warm water in bowl. Add honey. Mix. Cover for 2-3 minutes. Observe results.

Child should: Smell mixture. Tell what happens to mixture as yeast "works." Know that waiting is necessary to get results. Listen and watch as teacher shows air holes in bread caused by yeast.

Child learned: Yeast grows. You must wait to see it grow. Yeast makes bread grow. Mary put yeast into her bread so it would grow. She had to wait for the yeast to work in the bread.

Making Connections: Check for airholes caused by yeast in the bread you eat at home. Look at them through a magnifying glass. What other things do you wait for? How do you feel when you wait? How do you feel when what you've been waiting for happens?

Baking Barley Bread
(Recipe adapted from *Breads: Manna From Heaven*, Eileen Gaden, Chappaqua, N.Y.: Christian Herald Books.)

Materials: Large mixing bowl and spoon

1 T dry yeast	$1/4$ cup honey
$1/4$ cup warm water	$1/2$ t salt
pinch of ginger	$1/4$ cup coarse barley (grind in blender
3 or 4 drops honey	or processor)
1 cup sour milk, room temperature	1 $3/4$ cup barley flour (find in health food store)
$1/4$ cup oil	2 cups whole wheat flour

Procedure: Dissolve yeast, ginger, 3 or 4 drops honey in warm water. Cover and set aside for 5 minutes. In large bowl, mix sour milk, oil, honey, salt, coarse barley, and barley flour. Mix well. Stir in yeast mixture. Mix. Add 1 $1/2$ cups whole wheat flour and mix. Add remaining flour until dough cleans side of bowl. Knead 10 minutes. Place in greased bowl, cover, let rise 1 $1/2$ hours. Punch down. Let rise again 1 hour. Shape into 2 round loaves, 5 inches in diameter. Place on greased baking sheet, cover, and let rise 1 hour. Bake in 375 oven for about 30 minutes. Remove to rack. Rub with butter or margarine. Let cool. Break into bite-size pieces to serve.

> (NOTE) This procedure takes about 4 $1/2$ hours. A teacher might need to choose one part of this procedure to do with students—kneading, shaping, baking, or tasting. In this case, the next 3 sections need to be adjusted to fit individual teacher's procedures.

suggestion - 2½ hrs. prior to class, mix a batch of barley bread so it can be completed during class.

Child should: Touch and compare dough in sticky and smooth stages. Observe growth of dough caused by action of yeast. Smell bread baking. Break (not slice) bread into small pieces. Taste bread with butter or honey.

Child learned: Mary baked bread for her family. Jesus ate barley bread. You wait a lot when you bake bread. Bread smells wonderful when it's baking. It's fun to make something to eat.

Making Connections: How do you think Jesus might have helped Mary make bread? Have you ever helped make something to eat with your family? What did you do? Who did you help? How did you feel about waiting for it to be ready?

Making Butter

Materials: Half-pint glass jar with tight-fitting lid

$1/2$ cup whipping cream, room temperature
(Yield: $1/4$ cup butter)
(Approximate time: 10 minutes)

Procedure: pour cream into jar. Take turns shaking until butter appears. Pour off excess liquid. Taste with toothpicks or on bread.

Child should: Watch for changes in cream. Discover hands and arms might get tired.

Child learned: Mary made butter for her family. Making butter takes a long time. Doing something for others is sometimes hard work.

Making Connections: Who makes the food you eat? How could you help? How could you show you are thankful to the person who makes your food?

Tasting Corner

Materials: Figs, dates, apricots, almonds, walnuts, olives, and feta, pot, or farmer's cheese,—barley bread broken into bite-size pieces, butter, honey.

Procedure: Arrange foods so students can choose and taste leisurely.

Child should: Look at, smell, touch, taste foods. Tell which are sticky, sweet, hard, soft, chewy, etc.

Child learned: To name some foods Jesus ate. To taste some of those same foods. That new foods could taste good. To identify foods he or she liked or disliked and why.

Making Connections: What are some foods you like to eat? How do you feel about trying new foods? Which foods that Jesus ate do you have at home? Tell your family about the foods that Jesus ate that you like to eat, too.

Marketplace

Materials: Chopped figs, dates, apricots, raisins, walnuts, almonds, pistachios, spoon or scoop with each food, 1 small baby food jar with lid for each student, materials to decorate jar.

Procedure: Teacher will create a marketplace by aranging various foods on tables or desks. Children "buy" food to share with family. Layer desired food in baby food jars. Cover tightly. Decorate jar as desired.

Child should: Choose a variety of ingredients, note colors and textures, name foods chosen.

Child learned: To name and describe some of the foods Jesus ate. Food can be pretty. Food can be a gift.

Making Connections: Who will you share this gift of food with? How do you think they will feel about getting it? How will giving it make you feel? Who else could your family share food with?

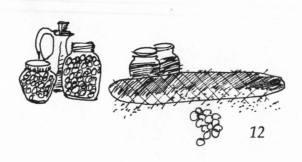

THE MAKING FOOD SONG

(tune: "Row, Row, Row Your Boat")

Crush, crush, crush the grain,
Pound with all your might!
And you will make barley flour
Smooth and soft and light.

Punch, punch, punch the dough,
Mix the yeast all through.
Then your dough will raise and be
Bread just right for you!

Shake, shake, shake the cream,
Shake it all around.
If you shake it long enough,
Butter will be found!

HOMES
Teacher's Page—Historical Background

First-century village homes in Galilee were small, box-like buildings, usually constructed from handmade, sun-dried clay brick or from stone. A low, narrow doorway led into the one-room structure. The living area doubled as kitchen and bedroom and was raised about eighteen inches. A lower level across the front of the room was used for storage and as an animal shelter. Animals were usually brought inside at night.

Clay and limestone chips were packed together to make a hard floor. In an effort to waterproof the walls, they were whitewashed with a lime plaster. A small window might be cut into the wall.

The flat roof was made of branches woven together, placed on rafters, and covered with clay that became a hard plaster from the heat of the sun. This plaster helped keep the rain out of the house. After a heavy rain, the father would use a heavy stone roller to spread the clay evenly over the branches again.

The roof, reached by a ladder, provided extra living space for the family. As a safety precaution, an eighteen-inch-high wall was erected around the perimeter. (See Deuteronomy 22:8.) On hot evenings, the family might eat or sleep on the roof. It was also the place for shouting news to neighbors, drying fruit or wet clothes, meditating, holding private talks, doing chores like spinning, or even adding another room.

Furnishings were sparse. One treasured item was the clay oil lamp, often the only source of light. It was kept in a special niche in the wall so it wouldn't get broken. Other furnishings might include a cookstove, cooking utensils, and a variety of pottery. Sleeping mats made of woven rushes were rolled up and placed out of the way during the day.

There were no bathrooms. Bodily cleansing was done in the courtyard or in the street so that the water being used wouldn't turn the house's floor into mud.

Houses offered little privacy and few material comforts, but these close, primitive quarters did provide the stability and security needed to support traditions and nurture the growth of the strong Jewish family unit.

(NOTE: Two excellent historically accurate teaching visuals, a cross-section of a Galilean home and a village scene, are published by Winston Press as part of the *Joy Alive* Program.)

Homes

Square
Clay bricks or stone
One story
One room
Animals inside at night
Sparsely furnished
Sleeping mats
Oil lamp
Walled roof
No bathroom

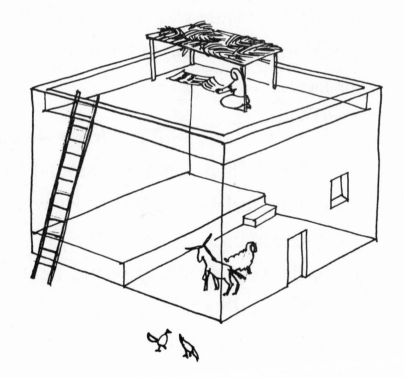

IN JESUS' HOUSE

If you lived in Jesus' house, you would eat and sleep in the same room! That's because there was just one room in his small square house. His family did everything together in that one room. The animals came inside at night!

Jesus didn't have a bed as you do. He slept on a woven mat on the floor. If he got cold, Mary covered him with his mantle. (A mantle was like a coat.) In the morning, Jesus would roll up his mat, put it away, and go outside to wash his face.

On hot days, Jesus and Mary would climb a ladder to the flat roof. There was a wall around the roof. On the roof, Jesus could feel the cool breeze. He would play while Mary did her spinning.

In the evening, Mary would light the oil lamp. Jesus and Mary and Joseph felt cozy as they watched the lamp make shadows on the wall. Jesus liked being close to his family.

Teacher's Page
Making Connections

Perhaps it's difficult to imagine the young Jesus living in a small, dark, crowded house that had poor ventilation and no modern conveniences. Yet it was a place that offered security, warmth, and peace. It was not only a shelter, but a place of love and respect.

From his crowded living conditions, Jesus might have learned how to share and keep things in order. As he watched Mary tend the oil lamp, he might have learned about light: how it illuminated, warmed, welcomed, dispelled fear. He would have witnessed the care and vigilance necessary to keep it. From the cozy companionship of family, he would have learned people are more important than things.

How can you help families make their homes places of security, warmth, and peace?

How can you make your classroom a warm and loving place?

Discussion/Activity Starters

Jesus and his family ate and slept in the same room. What places do you share with others? With whom? How does this make you feel?

Jesus helped put his mat away. How do you help in your home?

Mary lit the oil lamp each night. How do you get light in your house? How does light help you?

Jesus liked playing on the roof while Mary worked there. Where is your favorite place in your house? Why?

Jesus liked being with his family. What do you like to do with your family?

Activities

Clay Pottery Or Oil Lamps

Materials: Modeling clay

Procedure: Children knead and mold clay into a ball which can be shaped into a bowl or cup. Older children can make oil lamps by flattening the ball somewhat and making the oil well, then pinching it to form the beak-like portion that contains the wick. (A good photo of an oil lamp appears on p. 115, *Jesus and His Times*, Pleasantville, N.Y.: Reader's Digest Association.)

Child should: Feel and describe texture of clay.

Child learned: Jesus drank from a clay cup. Water was stored in big clay jars. Mary cooked and stored food in clay pots. Clay oil lamps were used for light. Clay utensils could be broken easily.

Making Connections: What do you drink from? What does your Mom put food in when she cooks? Where do you keep your water? What do your lamps look like? What's different about the lamp in Jesus' house? What's the same?

Woven Mats

Materials: Each child needs: 14" x 14" poster board

      six $1/2$" x 14" strips of poster board in various colors

      glue or tape

Procedure: Teacher prepares weaving project for each child: Leaving a 2 $1/2$" border, draw a 9" x 9" square in the center of 14" x 14" poster board. Inside the 9" x 9" square, draw perpendicular, intersecting lines $1/2$" apart to make thirty-six $1/2$" x $1/2$" squares. Cut seven 9" long vertical lines starting at outside edge of 9" x 9" square.

Children will weave their $1/2$" strips horizontally through the vertical cuts. Edges can be glued or taped in place. (To simplify weaving directions, mark an x over each square to be covered by paper strip.)

Child should: Notice patterns made by weaving. Discover that making things takes time and patience. Feel good about being able to make something useful.

Child learned: Jesus, Mary, and Joseph used mats to sleep on and to sit on while eating. We can make useful things.

Making Connections: What can you use your mat for in your house? Can you find other things in your house that are woven? Use your hands to make something else for your home.

J esus' House Treasure Hunt

Materials: Picture or drawings of items found in Jesus' house, such as: pottery, sleeping mat, cookstove, oil lamp, broom, ladder, donkey, etc.
Pictures of modern items, such as: TV, bed, lamps, vacuum cleaner, etc.

Procedure: Prior to class, teacher hides pictures around room. Students search to find one picture of an item found in Jesus' house. Bring to designated location.

Child should: Differentiate between biblical and modern items.

Child learned: To name and tell how biblical items were used.

Making Connections: Tell how you and Jesus used different things for the same purpose.

IN JESUS' HOUSE (Echo Pantomime)
(Students repeat lines and motions after teacher.)

Come, see my house! (motion to come in)

It's square like a box! (using index fingers, draw square in air)

Bend low to come inside. (bend low)

Here in the front, (point)

the donkey, goat, and chickens do abide. (pet each animal)

Climb one big step (step up)

and you will be where

I eat my meals and sleep. (eating motion, head on folded hands)

When the lamp is lit (light lamp)

I like to watch (watch)

the shadows sway and leap! (sway and leap)

Now climb the ladder (climb up)

to the roof. Sit (sit) in the shade of the wall. (fanning motion)

Here's where we sing (mouth open to sing) and laugh (laugh) and talk.
(pantomime talking)

It's the very best place of all! (cross hands over heart)

CLOTHING
Teacher's Page—Historical Background

The dress of the common people who lived in first century Galilee was loose-fitting, unornamented, and functional. Fabric, often produced in the home, was usually wool or linen left in its natural color. Pins, knots, and buttons were not generally used.

The inner garment for men was a short straight-lined tunic worn belted at the waist so it wouldn't get in the way while the wearer was working. The tunic was usually made from two pieces of coarsely woven naturally colored wool or linen sewn together at the shoulders and sides. Occasionally, one long piece of material was used, eliminating the need for shoulder seams. The belt was made from folded cloth or a strip of leather.

Another type of men's tunic was ankle length and straight-lined with slits on the sides at the hemline. Sometimes dyed with animal or vegetable dyes, this garment was worn indoors or outdoors when physical activity wasn't required.

The outer wear, called a mantle, was made of heavier wool and doubled as a covering at night. This garment was a large square cloth that was draped around the body or held close with a belt. As a reminder to follow God's law, Jewish men wore blue tassels attached to each corner of the square. (Deuteronomy 22:12 and Numbers 15:38-41). When the mantle was worn, two tassels would hang in front, and two in back.

An upper mantle, again a square of fabric but smaller than the outer mantle, was worn to protect the head from sun or rain. Head coverings were important because Palestine had hot summers and cold, windy winters. Men usually wore a turban which was a woven cap with bleached white linen cloth wrapped around it. Sometimes the head was covered by a simple square of cloth tied in place. In summer, hair and sweat might be kept off the face by a leather strip or rolled cloth tie. Some current textbooks picture the child Jesus and Joseph wearing yarlmukes, but these were not worn by Jewish males until the middle ages.

Because there were no pockets in garments, purses, shaped like a small bag and made of leather, were worn in the belt or in the bosom of the tunic.

Feet were protected by sandals made of leather strips attached to wooden soles.

Women's tunics were longer than men's and were often embroidered at the neck and breast. Two outer garments used by women were the upper mantle and a sack-like sleeveless mantle. The square shaped upper mantle covered the head and upper body and could be used as a veil, shawl, or, if belted, as a bag to carry small bundles placed in the bosom. In public women covered their hair and faces. Jewish women wore their hair long, often in braids.

Male and female children wore natural colored tunics, usually unbelted to give them more freedom. Girls' tunics were longer than boys'. The woolen mantle was worn as the outer garment. Children, like adults, wore protective head coverings. On their heads, girls wore a large cloth that the upper mantle wrapped around. Boys often wore a woven cap or a square cloth tied in place.

Although clothing was plain, it was functional, comfortable, and protective.

Clothing

Plain	Blue tassels on mantle
Functional	Upper mantle
Protective	Turban (men)
Wool or linen	Veil (women)
Natural color	Sandals
Tunic (inner)	Purse worn in belt
Mantle (outer)	

WHAT JESUS WORE

Do you like to keep treasures in your pockets? When Jesus was a boy, he had a little purse to put his treasures in because he didn't have any pockets! He didn't wear jeans and shirts like you do. He wore a tunic. It looked like a sack with openings for his head and arms. Sometimes he wore a belt around his tunic. He could tuck his purse into his belt.

Jesus didn't have a coat like you do. If he felt cold, he wrapped a warm mantle around his tunic. The mantle was a square woolen piece of cloth. His mantle could keep out the wind and the rain. When he slept, he used the mantle for a blanket.

Mary made the clothes Jesus wore. She might have put blue tassels, like the ones Joseph had, on Jesus' mantle. The tassels helped everyone remember that God said, "Always try to love everyone."

Teacher's Page
Making Connections

The child Jesus' clothes were plain, functional, and protective.

Today, even young students become overly preoccupied with designer labels. How can you help your students develop a sensible attitude towards clothing?

Jesus would have watched the many steps necessary to make a garment. From this, he might have learned perseverance. He saw Mary's delight in being able to clothe her family. This might have influenced the way he understood service. He experienced how necessary clothing was to protect the body. This could have heightened his sympathy for the poor. He observed the men wearing blue tassels. Perhaps this helped him understand "covenant."

How can you help children learn that providing clothing is one way parents say, "I love you"? What opportunities can you give your students to share clothing with the poor?

Discussion/Activity Starters

What did Jesus wear to keep him warm? What do you wear to keep you warm? Where did Jesus keep the special things he found? Where do you put the things you find?

How do you think Jesus felt when Mary gave him a new tunic? What do you think he said? How can you show you are thankful for the clothes you get?

Blue tassels reminded Jesus and his family that God loved them. What do you wear that reminds you of God's love?

Activities

Purse ("Leather")

Materials: Circle of brown or tan felt, 12" diameter

24" x 1/2" ribbon or a shoelace

Procedure: Teacher preparation for each child: cut eight pairs of 1" slashes perpendicular to and 1" from the outer edge of circle. Space pairs equally around circle. Each slash in the pair should be 3/4" from its mate. Children will weave ribbon through the slashes. Pull tight and tie to make purse.

Children should: find something to put into purse.

Children learned: Jesus' garments had no pockets. Purses were used to carry small objects. Purses were tucked into belt or bosom of tunic.

Making Connections: What things do you think Jesus put in his purse? How do you think he felt when he found them? Have you found some of the same kinds of things? What else have you found? Where do you keep them? Do you show them to anyone? Who? Why?

Blue Tassels

(Enlist the help of several aids to help children tie tassels.)

Materials: 5" x 4" cardboard

Blue yarn - one 12" piece; one 18" piece; 9 yds, wound into a ball

Tape

Procedure: Wind 9 yards of yarn around cardboard lengthwise. (Make this easier for young children by taping down beginning end of yarn.) Slide 12" piece under all wound yarn at the top and tie securely. Slide off cardboard. About 1/2" down from top, wind 18" piece around all yarn and tie securely. Cut through all wound yarn at the bottom. Attach tassel to corner of mantle.

Child should: Feel texture of yarn. Hold cardboard with one hand, wind with the other. Count each rotation (approximately 32).

Child learned: Blue tassels were attached to mantles to remind people to follow God's law.

Making Connections: What kinds of things do you wear to remind you about God? What do they help you remember to do?

Easy Costume Ideas

(Once you get children started, they'll use their own imaginations to make costumes.)

Tunic: 2 plain pillow cases, pinned at the shoulders.

Belts: cord, yarn, or strips of fabric.

Mantle: plain tablecloth, baby blanket, fabric square, bath towel. Blue tassels can be stapled to corners.

Upper mantle for girls: plain large towel, tablecloth, scarf or fabric square.

Headdress for boys: plain pillowcase or receiving blanket to cover head. Tie on with men's large handkerchief rolled diagonally.

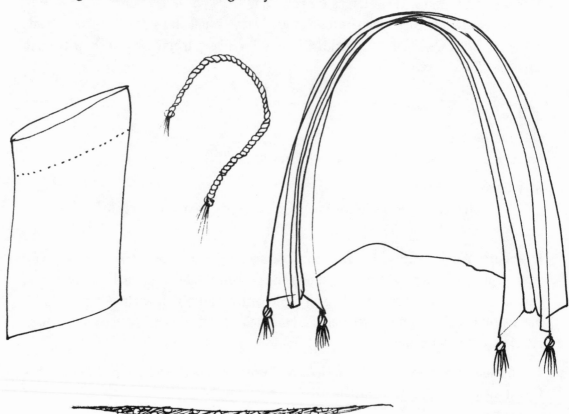

COSTUME PARADE

(While wearing their costumes, children make up motions as they say the following verses.)

My tunic has no collar,

Nor any pockets, neither.

But that's O.K. because, you see,

I really don't need either!

To keep my neck and shoulders warm,

I wrap my mantle 'round me.

It keeps me snug and dry, and so,

No storm has ever found me!

Instead of pockets to fill up,

When I explore at leisure,

I have a purse tucked in my belt

In which I keep my treasure!

My tunic has no collar,

Nor any pockets, neither.

But that's O.K. because, you see,

I really don't need either!

WORK
Teacher's Page—Historical Background

Jews of the first century viewed work as an honor and duty. Through their work they showed obedience to their God and Creator, who also was a worker. They strongly believed all people should have a skill enabling them to earn their daily bread. Even scholars worked at daily trades to support themselves. Children were expected to do their share of the work. At age five or six, boys began to learn their father's trade, while girls were taught domestic chores by their mothers. Idleness was not an acceptable way of life to the Jews.

The work day for a typical Jewish wife and mother would have started at sunrise and continued until evening, as she provided for the needs of her family. A trip to the well for fresh water would be made at least twice during the day. First, a leather bucket was used to lift the water from the well. Then the water was poured into a clay jug which the woman carried on her head. At home, the water would be poured into a large clay storage jug.

Much of a woman's day was spent preparing food. (See chapter on food.) She also

gathered twigs, branches, and dung for fuel. Another important job was making the family's clothing. This entailed washing the fleece, spinning thread, weaving cloth, and sewing. Washing clothes was a long process that required carrying the laundry to a nearby stream, wetting and rubbing it with home-made soap, beating it with a stick, kneading, rinsing, and spreading it to dry on a rock or on the roof. Sweeping the hard clay floor, filling the oil lamp, caring for the animals, and nurturing children were also part of a woman's daily tasks.

The father would have spent most of his day at his trade or in the field. A carpenter would have to saw trees into boards so he could make plows, yokes, small tables, wooden doors, and frames. With his bow-lathe he could turn spindles and bowls. Perhaps he carved wooden animals for the children. According to Jewish custom, a man would be expected to train his sons in his own trade. A man's home chores included rolling the roof after a heavy rainstorm. It was also the father's duty to teach his family the Torah and traditions of the Jewish faith.

The hustle and bustle of people at work permeated the village and surrounding areas. There were farmers, fishermen, herdsmen, gardeners, potters, smiths, tanners, tent makers, fullers, cloth dyers, bakers, cheesemakers, and butchers. Others were beekeepers, barbers and physicians, midwives, tax collectors, bankers, brickmakers, shoemakers, innkeepers, merchants, and laborers who could be hired by the day or the hour. The people of Galilee were a hard working people, proud of the skills that enabled them to perform honest work and to obey the Creator.

Work
    viewed as honor and duty
    everyone worked
    idleness not accepted
    children did chores
    fathers trained sons
    mothers trained daughters

JESUS WAS A HELPER

Jesus looked around and saw many people working. He saw farmers and fishermen. He saw people making pots and tents. He wanted to be a worker, too.

Jesus did many jobs to help Mary and Joseph. He might have fed the donkey or the chickens. Maybe he helped Mary carry water from the well. Baking bread was a big job for Mary. Jesus might have helped to grind the grain or knead the dough. Maybe he helped to spread the wet, clean clothes on bushes to dry.

When Jesus was five or six, he went to the carpenter shop to help Joseph. Joseph used wood to make plows and tables and doors and bowls. He used a tool called a plane to make the wood smooth. Maybe Jesus helped Joseph carry the wood he needed. Or maybe he swept up the curly wood shavings that fell from the plane.

Jesus was glad to help Mary and Joseph. He knew they were happy to have his help.

Teacher's Page
Making Connections

Try to picture the child Jesus eagerly working to help his family. Like other Jewish children, he was taught that working was a way to honor God. He must have been happy to know that he could show obedience to God by helping those he loved.

How can you encourage parents to give children opportunities to be helpful members of their families?

By modeling Mary and Joseph and others in his community, Jesus could have learned to be industrious. Doing daily chores would have taught him obedience and responsibility. Seeing Mary and Joseph work to care for their family would have taught him about love. Watching the villagers at their work might have taught him perseverance and patience.

What jobs can you give children in your classroom to help them learn responsibility?

Discussion/Activity Starters

Jesus helped Mary and Joseph. How did he help? Do you do any of the same things?

What other things do you do to help at home?

Jesus watched many workers in his village. Name some workers in your neighborhood.

Mary and Joseph taught Jesus to do many things. What have your parents taught you? Can you teach someone else to do those things?

What do you think Jesus' favorite job might have been? What is your favorite job? Why?

Activities

Carpenter Shop

Materials: small hand plane
block of soft wood
drop cloth to cover work area

Procedure: Each child takes a turn to plane wood. An adult should supervise each worker to insure safety.

Child should: Feel and smell the curly shavings. Notice the change in the wood as it is planed.

Child learned: Joseph planed wood to make it smooth. Jesus learned to plane wood. Planing makes curly shavings. Jesus might have swept up the shavings. Wood has a special smell.

Making Connections: Did anyone at your house ever make something from wood? What? Were you able to help? Name some ways you have helped someone make something. How did you feel about being helpful? How do you think Jesus felt about being helpful?

Curly Lambs

Materials: Outline of a lamb drawn on construction paper
curly shavings from planed wood
glue

Procedure: Cover lamb outline with glue. Sprinkle shavings on glue. Pat down gently. Dry.

Child should: Feel and smell wood shavings.

Child learned: Curly shavings were the scraps from the wood Joseph planed. Jesus might have played with them or swept them up to help Joseph.

Making Connections: Did you ever make something out of scraps before? Tell about it. Did you ever help someone clean up after they made something? Were they glad you helped? How do you think Joseph felt when Jesus helped?

Helper's Pantomime

Procedure: Seat children in a circle. Teacher or aid will stand in center and pretend to be "Mary." Each child will have a turn to be "Jesus." "Mary" will ask for help with a chore authentic to her time, saying, "Jesus, will you help me _____(name a chore.) (Teacher will explain unfamiliar words and motions.) "Jesus" will come to the center and say, "Yes, Mother, I will help you." "Mary" and "Jesus" will pantomime the action together. "Mary" will give each helper a smile, a hug, and a "thank you."

Chores to include: grind the grain, spin the wool, milk the goat, feed the donkey, gather twigs for the fire, punch milk to make butter, draw the water, sweep the floor, wash the clothes, knead the dough.

Fingerplay
CARPENTER 'S HAMMER

The carpenter's hammer goes tap-tap-tap,
(Pound right fist on left.)

His saw goes see-saw-see.
("Saw" right hand across left arm.)

He hammers and saws from morning till night,
(Alternate "hammering" and "sawing.")

Making a stool for me.
(Indicate stool with hands.)
(Add other stanzas for making a table, cart, plow, etc.)

PLAY
Teacher's Page—Historical Background

Playtime was limited in first-century Galilee because all available hands, including those of children, were needed to perform the chores necessary for sustaining daily life. Children did find ways to entertain themselves, however, after their chores were completed.

Races were popular, as were games similar to our hopscotch and jacks. Ball was played in the street or in the marketplace. Children played with animals in the courtyard of their homes or with puppies, often kept as house pets. Toys included whistles, rattles, wheeled animals, hoops, and spinning tops. Children could go exploring in both countryside and village where they could watch farmers tending crops or craftsmen working. They could discover interesting cloud formations and lovely natural views.

Older children and adults sometimes found time for board games, including a kind of chess. Younger children relied on memory and imagination as they re-enacted weddings, funerals, and festival celebrations.

For instance, they might have imitated the Sabbath ritual with its special food, clothing, and prayers or one of the pilgrimage festivals, complete with singing, dancing, feast-

ing, and travelling with family and friends. Impressed by the professional wailers and the sight of a body prepared for burial and carried on a bier in a funeral procession, children might have copied this ritual in their own play.

The colorful, lively wedding ceremony might have supplied many ideas the children could adapt as they played at being grown-up. In a Jewish wedding, the bride was dressed in elaborately embroidered clothes and jewels and coins, some dangling from a chain or ribbon tied around her forehead. The groom and all his attendants carried torches and went to the bride's house. After a joyful public greeting, they escorted her and all her attendants, who carried lamps, to the groom's house for the wedding feast. The wedding party was accompanied by the guests who sang and danced and played musical instruments as they processed.

Music, singing, and dancing were popular in daily life and religious festivals. Lyres, harps, flutes, horns, cymbols, drums, and tambourines were used to help people express and share their emotions.

Play in the time of Jesus' childhood, just as in our time, both reflected and passed on the culture of the day.

Toys	Games
whistles	races
rattles	ball
wheeled animals	jacks
hoops	hopscotch
tops	chess
musical instruments	exploring
	dress-up

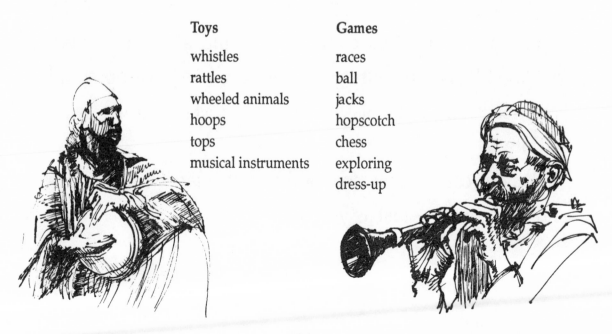

JESUS HAD FUN

Do you like to play "dress-up" or pretend you are "grown up"? When Jesus was your age, he probably liked to do those things, too. He liked to run races and play ball with his friends.

Maybe Jesus and his friends looked at the sky and saw pictures in the clouds. Perhaps they went exploring to find "treasures." They might have found "treasures" like these: bird's nest, feather, bird's egg, pretty flowers, shiny stone, or colored leaf. How many of those treasures can you find?

Jesus liked his toys. He had little wooden animals on wheels and a top that could spin round and round very quickly. Maybe he counted to see how long his top could spin! He might have played a song for Mary on his drum or flute.

When Jesus was a boy, he liked to play with his toys and his friends — just as you do!

Teacher's Page
Making Connections

Imagine the wonder in Jesus' eyes when he found an exquisite flower, a shiny, smooth stone, a brightly colored butterfly. Think of his laughing face as he ran races, scampered over the hillside, or played ball with his friends.

What activities can you plan that will offer your students similar experiences to enjoy?

From his exploration of the Palestinian countryside, Jesus could have learned of the uniqueness of all created things. He would have sensed the order and majesty of the Creator and felt appreciation for his gifts. By observing and imitating adults, he could have learned the traditions of the community. Playing with friends would have provided opportunities to share and learn about others.

Play is the way children learn about themselves and the world. What games can you play to teach students about the wonders of nature? How can you use play to help students understand themselves? Others?

Discussion/Activity Starters

Name some of the games Jesus might have played. Which of those have you played? What are some other favorite games of yours?

Jesus liked to dress up and play "wedding" or "festival." What do you play when you dress up?

If you could go to Jesus' house, what would you like to play with him? If Jesus could come to your house, what would you like to play?

Jesus liked to find interesting things in nature. Can you find something special to share?

Activities

Treasure Hunt

Materials: Treasures found in nature, such as robin's egg, feather, leaf, butterfly wing, bird's nest, shiny stone, flower, etc. (Note: more than one of each item could be used.)

Set of 3" x 5" cards (one card to picture or name each item)

treasure box

Procedure: Before class, teacher hides items. To insure that all experience success at finding an item, each child is given a 3" x 5" card naming an item to be found. If a child has difficulty finding an item, others can help search, but each child should carry an item to the treasure box.

Child should: Experience joy of discovery. Observe and touch beauty in nature.

Child learned: Jesus found treasures in nature. We have fun doing something Jesus did. God wants us to discover and enjoy all that he made.

Making Connections: Have you ever gone exploring? With whom did you share your treasure? Name some times when you can look for treasures in nature.

Musical Instruments

Lyre

Materials: Rectangular box with tight fitting lid. (A shoe or stationery box works well.)

2 pencils

4 rubber bands of various sizes

markers or poster paint

Procedure: Before class teacher cuts round hole (2" diameter) in center of each lid. Children decorate boxes with markers or poster paint. Stretch rubber bands across round hole. Insert pencils under rubber bands at opposite sides of hole to make bridge.

Cymbals

Materials: 2 aluminum pie pans

2 pieces of ribbon, 1 1/2" x 6"

colored tape

Procedure: Tape ribbon handles to back of pie pans.

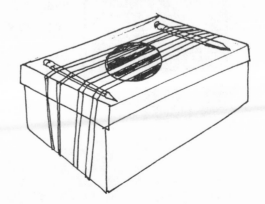

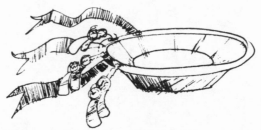

Tambourine

Materials: Plastic lid or shallow plastic container (8" across) or aluminum pie pan

3 pipe cleaners

6 rings from pop cans, light weight washers or paper clips

narrow ribbon for streamers

Procedure: Before class, teacher punches 3 holes equi–distant around circumference of lid, container, or pie pan. Children thread pipe cleaners through holes and attach rings, washers, or paper clips. Tie on streamers.

Horn

Materials: Stiff paper, tape, finger paint.

Procedure: Roll paper into cone shape, leaving small opening for mouth piece. Tape along seam. Children decorate with finger paint.

Drum

Materials: Round oatmeal box, plain paper, tape, markers, glue, glitter.

Procedure: Glue lid to box. Wrap paper around box and tape in place. Decorate with markers and glitter.

Child should: Choose an instrument to make. Experience making a toy. Have fun with their toy instrument.

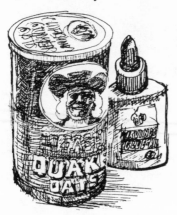

Child learned: To name some instruments Jesus was familiar with. Music was a part of Jesus' playtime.

Making Connections: When do you listen to music? Who listens with you? How does it make you feel? Did you ever make music by playing an instrument or singing? How did that make you feel?

THE MUSIC SONG

(Tune: "Frere Jacques")

We have fun,
We have fun,
With our drum,
With our drum!
Jesus had fun, too,
Just like we do!
With his drum,
With his drum!

(For additional verses, use lyre, cymbals, tambourine, horn. This can be used as a prayer activity by substituting, "We praise God" for the first two lines and "Jesus praised him, too" for line five.)

PRAYER
Teacher's Page—Historical Background

Jewish families living in Jesus' time believed prayer was an integral part of daily life. Because scripture governed all a person did, each moment of life had holy meaning and so blessings were recited before both ordinary and special happenings (washing hands, eating, dressing, performing chores, reading scripture, etc.). A typical blessing praised God as the supreme being and acknowledged man's dependance on God. This is illustrated in the blessing said over the bread: "Blessed art Thou, Lord, our God, King of the universe, who brings forth bread out of the earth."

The central creed of Judaism was proclaimed in the Shema (Deuteronomy 6:4-9, 11:13-21) which begins, "Hear, O Israel, the Lord, our God, the Lord is one." (Shema is Hebrew for "hear.") This belief set the Israelites apart from pagan cultures which believed in many gods. It kept them unified, even when they were forced to live apart in bondage or under foreign rule. The Shema was the first prayer a child learned and the last said by the dying. It was recited at rising and at bedtime in addition to being said with formal and informal prayers throughout the day.

As commanded in Deuteronomy 6:9, the Shema was written on a small scroll (mezuzah), placed in a box, and attached to the door post of every Jewish home. The mezuzah was reverently touched upon entering and leaving a home as a reminder of God's love and an encouragement to choose God's way. Some scholars say it came to symbolize the belief that the home was guarded by God's Word.

The Sabbath, or Shabbat, was a 24-hour period lasting from sundown on Friday to

sundown on Saturday when no work was permitted. This time was set aside for rest, prayer, and study of scripture. Three sharp blasts of the ram's horn announced the beginning of Shabbat on Friday and called the villagers to the synagogue for prayer. After the synagogue service, families returned home for a meal of special foods that had been prepared before Shabbat began. Blessings were said over the candles, the wine, and the bread. As they ate, families retold stories of God's goodness and enjoyed their rest and each other's company.

On Saturday morning, villagers returned to the synagogue for prayer and readings from the Torah or law (the first five books of Hebrew scripture). The Torah was written on a scroll made of pieces of parchment or papyrus that had been sewn together. The scroll was rolled around two rods called "trees of life" and kept in a wooden chest called an ark. The Torah was written in Hebrew with characters going from right to left. When it was read aloud, the scroll was placed on a table and unwound from the left side onto the right side. It could be read by any male member of the congregation. Immediately after the reading in Hebrew, it was translated into Aramaic, the common language of the time. The Shabbat service included several readings from the Torah, commentary, a reading from the prophets, and blessings.

Studying the Torah was a form of worship and a life long obligation. Fathers were responsible for teaching the law to their children, both by word and example. After a boy reached age five or six, he would attend a formal school where he would memorize the words and lessons of Torah.

Three times a year, during the Feast of Booths, Feast of Weeks, and Passover, male Jews were required to worship at the temple in Jerusalem. Many times their families travelled with them. Music, furnished by cymbals, stringed instruments, trumpets, drums, and tambourines, was an important part of temple ceremonies and Jewish worship. Woman often played tambourines, sometimes called hand drums, to beat time for singing during processions and festivals. The psalms were written to be sung, and we can assume that Jesus, Mary, and Joseph, being faithful Jews, sung them repeatedly.

Prayer Customs

One God—central belief	Torah is God's law
Shema—first prayer child learned	Torah written on scroll in Hebrew
Blessings said throughout day	Torah translated into Aramaic
Sabbath—24 hours, no work	Three pilgrimage festivals
Sabbath—rest, prayer, scripture	Music important form of worship

JESUS LIKED TO PRAY

Do you like having someone read to you? Jesus did, too! But Jesus didn't have books like you do. When Jesus was a boy, stories were written on scrolls. Scrolls were made from animal skins or heavy paper. They were written on and rolled up. Instead of turning pages, Jesus would unroll a scroll to read a story.

Jesus liked to hear stories about God. It made him feel good to know how much God loved him. You can find the stories Jesus liked to hear in your Bible! When you go to Mass, you will hear some of those stories being read!

Jesus liked to talk to God. He could tell God when he was happy and when he was sad. Jesus knew he could talk to God all through the day.

Jesus liked to sing and play music to show God how much he loved God. Do you have a song you can sing to praise God?

Teacher's Page
Making Connections

Think of the peace and security the child Jesus must have felt when he prayed. Raised in Jewish tradition, he was taught from his earliest years that each moment of life was holy and that God was always true to his promises.

What can you do to make students comfortable about speaking and listening to God?

Jesus heard and read and touched and said the Shema many times a day. From this he learned that one God was creator of the universe. Jesus listened as scripture stories were read and re-read. This taught him about God's steadfast love. From Sabbath celebrations, Jesus learned to love God's Word.

What different kinds of prayer opportunities can you give your students? What can you do to encourage families to pray together?

Discussion/Activity Starters

Jesus liked to talk to God all through the day. When do you pray? What do you say?

Sometimes Jesus sang to say, "Thank you, God." Sing a song that shows your praise or thanks to God.

The first prayer that Jesus learned is in your Bible. Be a detective and find it! Someone who is older can help you. (Deuteronomy 6:4-9) Ask someone to tell you what it means.

By praying and listening, Jesus learned what God wanted him to do. Who can help you learn what God wants you to do?

Activities

Scrolls

Materials: 2 drinking straws

tape

parchment type paper, 4 1/2" x 11", with Deuteronomy 6:4 printed in easily traceable letters along 11" edge

1 piece of yarn or ribbon, 12"

Procedure: Older children tape straws to 4 $1/2$" ends of paper, roll inward to center, and tie with yarn or ribbon. Younger children receive finished scroll, untie, unroll, and trace letters.

Child should: Roll and unroll scrolls. Read and/or trace words of Shema.

Child learned: Scrolls were the "books" of Jesus' time. Scrolls were held with rods upright; message appeared horizontally as scroll was unrolled. Shema was the first prayer Jesus learned. There is one God who loves us all.

Making Connections: When do you pray? Do you have a favorite prayer? Look in the Bible to find the first prayer Jesus learned. What things in your home remind you that God loves you and wants you to love everyone?

Classroom Scroll

Materials: 2 rods for scroll ends (cardboard papertowel rolls, broom handles, dowels, etc.)

drawing paper for each child

crayons or markers

tape

yarn or ribbon

Procedure: Position paper with long side at bottom. Each child writes a prayer and illustrates it. (Teacher or aid can write words as child dictates.) Connect drawings at sides with tape to make one long piece. Tape rods to first and last piece. Roll towards center and tie to make one large scroll. Use in prayer service of "Shabbat Table" activity. Each child reads own prayer from scroll. Other children answer "Amen."

Child should: Compose prayer. Illustrate prayer. Lead prayer. Listen to other prayers. Respond "Amen."

Child learned: Jesus heard prayers and stories read from scrolls. Rods were held upright; message was revealed as paper was unrolled horizontally. Jesus prayed with Mary and Joseph at home and with many people in the synagogue. We share prayers with others.

Making Connections: Where do you hear prayer? What are some books that have prayer in them? With whom do you share prayer? When you hear Bible stories at Mass, remember that Jesus heard some of the same stories in the synagogue.

Hebrew Language

(If you live near a Hebrew school, ask for permission to have some children tape several blessings in Hebrew. The Shabbat blessings over bread and wine work well for this activity.)

Materials: cassette tape of Jewish children reciting blessings in Hebrew.

Procedure: Explain that Jesus prayed in Hebrew. Tell the children that this is a prayer he might have said and this is how his language sounded. Play tape. Read English translation and explain that this is what is being said. Ask them to close their eyes and imagine the child Jesus praying. Play tape again.

Child should: Hear Hebrew language spoken.

Child learned: Jesus prayed in Hebrew. Prayers can be said in different languages. We can mean the same thing, even though different words are used.

Making Connections: At Mass, the priest says blessings over the bread and wine. They are much like the Hebrew blessings on the tape recording. Two Hebrew words we use when we pray are "Amen" (I believe) and "Alleluia" (Praise Yahweh). Do you know anyone who speaks another language? Can you understand everything they say? Do you like them, even if you don't always understand them?

Shabbat Table

Materials: prayer table, table cloth, flowers, candles, pretty dishes and cups, bread, fruit, juice

Procedure: Ritualize this procedure so children will feel its importance. Play soft music as each child places one object on table. Classroom Scroll prayer activity, Bible reading, and food are shared after table is prepare.

Child should: Work together to set eye-pleasing table.

Child learned: Jesus' family celebrated day of rest called Shabbat each week. They prayed, ate special food at a pretty table, rested, heard stories about God.

Making Connections: When do you celebrate a special meal? Who is with you? Are there special dishes and foods? How do you feel about being at a special meal? The Mass is a special meal we celebrate each Sunday. With whom do you go to Mass? What do you see, hear, and do there?

SONG PRAYER
(This activity uses Carey Landry's "Thank You, God," *Hi, God 1.*)

Materials: drawing paper, markers or crayons, cassette, and recorder to teach song.

Procedure: Children identify something they are thankful for. Draw and label. Young children will need help with labeling. Children sing "Thank You, God." Each takes a turn finishing the phrase, "For giving us..."

Child should: Take turns showing picture and identifying what they are thankful for at appropriate time in song.

Child learned: Singing is a way to pray. Jesus sang prayers called Psalms.

Making Connections: How do you feel about singing? When are some times you sing to pray? Who sings with you? Can you learn a new songprayer? Can you teach it to someone?

SUKKOT (Feast of Booths)
Teacher's Page—Historical Background

Sukkot is the Hebrew name for the Feast of Booths or Tabernacles. (Sukkot is plural for sukkah which means "covering" or "shelter.") It is one of the three pilgrimage feasts, along with Passover and the Feast of Weeks, that male Jews were commanded to celebrate in Jerusalem.

Rules for celebrating Sukkot are found in Exodus 23:16, Leviticus 23:34–36 and 23:42–43, Numbers 29:12–38, and Deuteronomy 16:13–15. This seven day festival marked the fruit harvest at the end of the year and was to begin on the fifteenth day of Tishri, the seventh month of the Jewish calendar (which corresponds to our early October). Sukkot was a time for living in booths, praising God, and rejoicing. Scholars say the booths recall both the temporary dwellings of the Israelites during the Exodus and the huts of field workers who gathered the autumn harvest.

The three most important commandments regarding this festival were to live in a sukkah for a week, to gather the four species (citron, palm, myrtle, and willow) for use in praising the Creator, and to rejoice.

Those who could traveled to Jerusalem and built a sukkah there. Others might have put up their sukkah on the roof of their house or in the street. The sukkah was a three-sided temporary dwelling. The roof had to be organic in nature, woven loosely so that the stars could be seen through it. The sukkah was to be decorated in a way that would be welcoming and beautiful. As much as possible, natural items such as fruit, vines, and flowers were used to decorate the sukkah. Each family literally moved into its sukkah for a week. People ate, slept, studied scripture, and welcomed friends there.

Worship in the temple included a ritual procession in which the celebrants car-

ried a citron in their left hand and palm, myrtle, and willow branches in their right. These were waved in the four directions of the wind and up and down to signify God's surrounding presence. Rejoicing continued into the night as the pilgrims danced before bonfires and torch light.

Several themes emerged from the celebration of Sukkot. One, illustrated by the temporary dwelling, was impermanance and dependence on God. The second theme was hospitality and the sharing of simple pleasures, symbolized by the open side of the dwelling. Thanksgiving for the harvest and all of God's gifts was a third theme. The major theme of joy was carried out as people rested from work, praised God for his bounty, and made merry for a week because "God has blessed you in all your crops and in all your undertakings" (Deuteronomy 16:15).

Sukkot Customs
Feast of Booths

travel to Jerusalem	live in sukkah for 7 days
build sukkah	gather 4 species
3-sided temporary dwelling	ritual procession
loosely woven roof	rest, rejoice, give thanks

A REMEMBERING PARTY

For many years, Jesus' ancestors had no country. They walked through hot, dry land looking for a place to live. Every night they took branches and built little booths to sleep in. God always stayed with them and fed them and protected them.

After they found their land, God wanted everyone to remember how God had watched over them. So every year they had a big party. It was called the "Feast of Booths" because every family built a little booth and lived in it for a week.

Jesus helped Mary and Joseph get ready for the party. He helped build the booth. (In Hebrew, it was called a sukkah.) He helped decorate it with flowers and vines and fruit and vegetables. He wanted it to look pretty.

Jesus and his family ate and slept in their sukkah for a whole week! Joseph would tell stories. They could see the stars through the leafy roof! Jesus felt very cozy in his family's sukkah!

Making Connections

How excited Jesus must have been as Sukkot approached. The entire village bustled as people prepared to travel to Jerusalem or celebrate at home. Imagine the laughter and talk and music and smiles and colors that must have accompanied the preparations.

What multi-sensory activities can you do to put your students in a festive mood?

Jesus watched as the harvest was gathered and people prepared to celebrate Sukkot. This might have deepened his understanding of covenant. He heard the Exodus story which taught about God's steadfast love. Staying in the sukkah with Mary and Joseph could have made him feel secure. He saw the varied colors of the harvest and the sukkah decorations. This might have helped him to appreciate the splendor of God's gifts. Jesus was a part of a rejoicing community. From this he could have learned that God wants us to be happy.

Discussion/Activity Starters

What do you think Jesus did to help get ready for the Feast of Booths? What do you do to help your family get ready for parties?

Jesus felt cozy in the sukkah with Mary and Joseph. When do you feel cozy?

Ask someone in your family to tell a story about a time God helped them.

Jesus and his family were happy to praise God. What do you thank God for? When can you and your family praise God together?

Building A Sukkah

(Teachers prepare sukkah. Children decorate them. Divide class into families and build a sukkah for each "family." Build enough sukkot so that each family will fit comfortably inside its sukkah.)

Materials: large appliance box (roof and 1 side cut away)
or table turned on end (fabric or cardboard for walls)
green crepe paper strips, lattice lumber, or yard sticks for roof.

Procedure: Sukkah should have 3 sides and an open roof. Weave crepe paper or place lumber on top to make lattice-like roof.

Decorating the Sukkah

Materials: patterns of fruit, colored paper, markers, crayons or paint, scissors, thread and needle, cranberries or popcorn, tissue paper, fall flowers, pumpkins or gourds.

Procedure: Children make paper fruit, paper chains, tissue flowers; they string cranberries and popcorn; they arrange flowers and vegetables to decorate sukkah.

Child should: Notice colors, feel textures of materials, cooperate with others in decorating the sukkah.

Child learned: Jesus, Mary, and Joseph lived in a sukkah when they celebrated the Feast of Booths. Jesus might have helped decorate it. Many colors occur in nature. God created beautiful things.

Making Connections: Tell about a time when you helped to put up decorations at school or at home. How does helping make you feel?

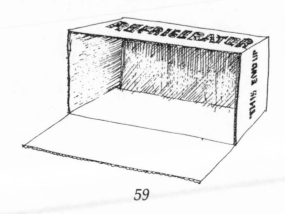

Sukkot Praises

Materials: A supple branch (willow, evergreen, or cornstalk) for each child.

Procedure: Children carry branches and move in a circle around sukkah while singing "Thank you, Lord" by Carey Landry (*Hi, God!*, vol. 1). Use "food," "homes," "being with us" in the verses. Stand in place at the chorus. Face north, south, east, west in time with the music. Tell the children that this shows we know God is everywhere.

Child should: Sing a song praising God. Walk to the beat of the music.

Child learned: Jesus used song and movement to pray. Song can be a prayer. Jesus prayed outside. God is everywhere. We thank God for all he gives us.

Making Connections: What are some different ways you pray? Where are some places you pray? Learn a song that you can sing with others at Mass.

Inside the Sukkah

Materials: sukkah, decorations, food (fresh fruit cut into bite-sized pieces).

Procedure: Children enter sukkah. Share food.

Child should: Enjoy coziness. Notice decorations. Share variety of food.

Child learned: Jesus, Mary, and Joseph were in the sukkah together. It's nice being with people we like. It's fun to share. Just as we are close to each other in the sukkah, God is close to us always. God takes care of us.

Making Connections: How do you think Jesus felt being in the sukkah with Mary and Joseph? What do you like about being in the sukkah? Where are some other places you feel cozy? How can you show people you like to be with them?

GAME—IN MY SUKKAH
(To be played inside sukkah.)

The first child says, "In my sukkah,

I'm eating————(name food)."

The next child repeats the sentence

and adds another food;

the third does the same, and so on,

until someone forgets or mixes up the order.

CHILDREN'S BLESSING
(Said by parents to children before the Shabbat supper.
From *Shabbat: A Peaceful Island*, Malka Drucker, N.Y.: Holiday House.)

May God bless you and keep you.

May God watch over you in kindness.

May God grant you a life of good health, joy, and peace.

SHAVUAT (Feast of Weeks)
Teacher's Page—Historical Background

Shavuat (Hebrew for "weeks") was one of the three pilgrimage feasts that male Jews were required to celebrate in Jerusalem each year. It took place seven weeks or fifty days after the second day of Passover, and so was celebrated in Sivan, the third month of the Hebrew calendar (our early May). In Jesus' day, it was often referred to by its Greek name, Pentekoste, and is the source of the Christian holy day, Pentecost. It also was known as the Festival of First Fruits because it commemorated the harvest of spring wheat and other produce.

Commandments governing the celebration of Shavuat are found in Exodus 23:16, Leviticus 23:15–21, Numbers 28:26–31, and Deuteronomy 16:9–12. For seven weeks, the Hebrews had been waiting as the wheat and fruit matured. Now Shavuat gave them an opportunity to thank God for a bountiful harvest. They traveled to the temple in Jerusalem, bringing with them a sheaf of wheat and a basket containing two loaves of bread made from the new wheat. Also in the basket was a free will offering of the first fruits of their crops of grapes, figs, pomegranates, olives, and dates.

Family members, carrying their offerings, walked together towards Jerusalem, through villages and over countrysides. Often they were led by a flute player. This was a joyful crowd, happy to have received God's gifts and ready to acknowledge their depen-

Mild Climate

dence on him through the designated ritual sacrifice at the temple.

The Jews were commanded to invite all to take part in this celebration and "make merry before the Lord...your son and daughter, your male and female slave, the Levite, the alien, the orphan and the widow" for, the Lord reminded the Hebrews, "you, too, were once slaves in Egypt" (Deuteronomy 16:11–12). This festival gave the Jews the opportunity to live the law as they shared food and companionship with the poor and the lonely.

The major theme of Shavuat was thanksgiving to God for providing food for mankind but, through the symbol of bread, it also celebrated the partnership between God and man in giving food to the world.

Shavuat Customs

Feast of Weeks	carried first fruit offerings
Pentekoste (Greek)	gave thanks to God
travelled to Jerusalem	rejoiced with family, poor, and lonely
carried bread made from new wheat	

A THANK YOU PARADE

When Jesus was a boy the families in his country were very happy that God had given them food. Every spring when the crops were ripe, they had a big parade and a party to tell God "Thank you." They called the party the "Feast of Weeks."

First they made bread from the new wheat. Then they picked the first ripe grapes, figs, pomegranates, olives, and dates. They put the best ones in a basket. They called all the people to help carry everything to the temple in Jerusalem. A temple is a very big beautiful building. People go there to pray. The temple was far away, but the people didn't mind. They sang and laughed and danced on the way. It was like a big parade!

At the temple the food was blessed and everyone thanked God for it. Then they had a party. They asked everyone who was lonely or poor to come to the party, too, because God wanted everyone to be happy! And everyone was happy because God loved them all!

Making Connections

To see the colors, hear the sounds, and smell the smells coming from a parade of happy people carrying their first fruits towards Jerusalem must have been an unforgettable adventure for young Jesus. This religious festival of Shavuat was truly a celebration.

What opportunities to praise the Lord using all their senses can you give your students?

Jesus saw an abundance of food being harvested. From this he might have learned that God provides for his people. He walked among people happily fulfilling their duty to thank God. This might have taught him it is right to praise the Lord. He saw the poor and lonely included in the festivities. From this he could have learned that God wants us to care for one another.

How can religious celebrations help families be joyful witnesses to God's commands in their daily lives? Can you take a celebration to a shut-in or rest home to give the lonely the opportunity to praise God in community?

Discussion/Activity Starters

Jesus' family and neighbors were so happy about the food God gave them that they had a parade to say, "Thanks!" What are some ways you show you are happy that God loves you?

God wants all people to be happy. Do you know people who are sad? What can you do to cheer them up?

Make something for people in a nursing home or hospital to remind them that God loves them.

Activities

Praise Parade

Materials: Invitations, sandwich boards, favors
> fruit salad (see below)
> musical instruments (see chapter on play)
> Easter baskets
> food for needy

Procedure: Children will parade in praise of God. Other students, families, friends, parishioners can be invited to join parade. Parade route could be in or around school or church. Paraders could carry baskets of food for needy or shut-in parishioners. Parade should end with a prayer service.

Child should: March and sing God's praises with others.

Child learned: Jesus and his family walked to Jerusalem to praise God. We have many things to thank God for. Giving God thanks and praise makes us feel happy. Lots of people like to give God thanks and praise. We can bring happiness to others.

Making Connections: Jesus and his family were happy to go to the temple to praise God. What are some ways you tell God of your love? How does that make you feel?

Invitations

Materials: colored paper
> stickers or pictures cut from catalogs or magazines
> markers
> glue
> insert containing parade information (date, time, place, what to bring)

Procedure: Fold paper in half. On front, teacher will write, "Join our Praise Parade! Help me thank God for...." Students will finish sentence by listing things they are thankful for. Younger students can identify these by using stickers or pre-cut pictures. Insert can be glued or stapled inside.

Child should: Identify things to be thankful for. Share list with others.

Child learned: God gives us many things. We are dependent on God. We can ask others to join us in praise.

Making Connections: Jesus and his family thanked God for giving them food. What things can you thank God for? With whom can you share these things: a smile, a handshake, time?

Sandwich Boards

Materials: 1 piece 22" x 28" poster board for each child
pictures of fruit, vegetables, flowers
ribbon
markers
glue
hole punch

Procedure: Cut poster board in half. Students will decorate each half with pictures of fruit, vegetables, flowers. The words "Praise the Lord!" or "Give thanks to the Lord!" should appear on the signs. Punch holes near the top at shoulders so signs can be connected with ribbon. Children will wear sandwich boards in parade.

Child should: Identify gifts of the Creator.

Child learned: God gives us many things. It is good to praise God.

Making Connections: As Jesus and his family walked to Jerusalem, many people along the way saw that they praised God. People will see your Praise Parade. What will they learn from you?

Favors

(Inexpensive items that are purchased or made by hand can serve as favors to be given to spectators or participants. Favor suggestions: paper flowers, balloons, buttons, dried fruit in plastic wrap, book markers. Following are directions for a simple book marker.)

Materials: calendars (use the kind with boxes drawn around numbers)
scissors
floral gift wrap
glue
clear contact paper
verse printed on white paper: "Praise God all the weeks of your life!"

Procedure: Children will cut a one-week strip from calendar and glue this to wrong side of floral paper. Trim around calendar. Center and glue verse to floral side. Lay on clear contact paper. Fold contact over so other side of marker is covered. Trim.

Child should: Make something for others.

Child learned: Jesus went to Jerusalem during the Feast of Weeks. We should praise God always. We can encourage others to praise God.

Making Connections: Joseph and Mary taught Jesus to give thanks and praise to God. Who taught you? Can you teach someone else to praise and thank God? How will you do that?

First Fruit Salad

Materials: grapefruit or melon half for each group of 4 children; bite-sized pieces of fresh, firm fruit; toothpicks.

Procedure: Place grapefruit or melon half on plate, cut side down. Put bite-sized piece of fruit on toothpick and insert into rind of melon or grapefruit. Continue until rind is completely covered.

Child should: Prepare a snack for all to share. Notice colors, textures, smells of various fruits.

Child learned: God made many different fruits. Fruits are beautiful. Farmers take care of fruit so it will grow properly. Making something for someone is fun. Making something for someone makes us feel good.

Making Connections: Are there plants in your home or yard that you help to take care of? How do you help prepare food at home? How can you and your family thank God for the food you eat? With whom can you share your food?

Additional Reading List

Barclay, William. *Jesus of Nazareth*. Nashville: Thomas Nelson Publishers, 1981.

Black, Naomi, ed. *Celebration: The Book of Jewish Feasts*. New York: E.P. Dutton, 1987

Drucker, Malka. *Shabbot: A Peaceful Island*. New York: Holiday House, 1983.

Drucker, Malka, *Sukkot: A Time to Rejoice*. New York: Holiday House, 1982.

Gaden, Eileen. *Breads: Manna From Heaven*. Chappaqua, N.Y.: Christian Herald Books, 1977.

Greenberg, Judith and Helen H. Carey. *Jewish Holidays*. New York: Franklin Watts, 1984.

The Israelites. New York: Time-Life Books, 1975.

Jesus and His Times. Pleasantville, NY: Readers Digest Assoc., Inc., 1987.

Lazar, Wendy. *The Jewish Holiday Book*. Garden City, NY: Doubleday, 1977.

Purdy, Susan Gold. *Jewish Holidays*. New York: J.B. Lippincott Co., 1969.

Terringo, Robert J. *The Land and People Jesus Knew*. Minneapolis, Minn.: Bethany House Publishers, 1985.

Van Deursen, A. *Illustrated Dictionary of Bible Manners and Customs*. New York: Bell Publishing Co., 1989.